Successful Business

A 5-Steps System for Collecting and Keeping Your Customers

Azione Business

© Copyright 2022 - Azione Business - All rights reserved.

The following Book is reproduced below with the goal of providing information that is as accurate and reliable as possible. Regardless, purchasing this Book can be seen as consent to the fact that both the publisher and the author of this book are in no way experts on the topics discussed within and that any recommendations or suggestions that are made herein are for entertainment purposes only. Professionals should be consulted as needed prior to undertaking any of the action endorsed herein.

This declaration is deemed fair and valid by both the American Bar Association and the Committee of Publishers Association and is legally binding throughout the United States.

Furthermore, the transmission, duplication, or reproduction of any of the following work including specific information will be considered an illegal act irrespective of if it is done electronically or in print. This extends to creating a secondary or tertiary copy of the work or a recorded copy and is only allowed with the express written consent from the Publisher. All additional right reserved.

The information in the following pages is broadly considered a truthful and accurate account of facts and as such, any inattention, use, or misuse of the information in question by the reader will render any resulting actions solely under their purview. There are no scenarios in which the publisher or the original author of this work can be in any fashion deemed liable for any hardship or damages that may befall them after undertaking information described herein.

Additionally, the information in the following pages is intended only for informational purposes and should thus be thought of as universal. As befitting its nature, it is presented without assurance regarding its prolonged validity or interim quality. Trademarks that are mentioned are done without written consent and can in no way be considered an endorsement from the trademark holder.

Table of Content

Introduction 9

Chapter 1 13

Improving Your Mindset to Improve Your Business 13

Chapter 2 17

First Steps 17

Chapter 3 21

The Courage to Change 21

Chapter 4 27

Analyze What You Do 27

Chapter 5 33

When You Can't Stay in Business 33

Chapter 6 37

I Was Missing an Important Piece 37

Chapter 7 ....
41

Finding the Right Solutions ....
41

Chapter 8 ....
47

Let's Take Action with My 5-Steps Method ....
47

Part 1: You ....
47

Step 1: Mindset ....
49

Step 2: Routine ....
55

Step 3: Act ....
63

Part 2: Your Business ....
73

Step 4: Acquire New Customers ....
75

Step 5: Loyal Recurring Customers ....
92

Chapter 9 ....
111

How to Improve the Process ....
111

Chapter 10 ....
117

What to Do Now? 117

Conclusion 121

Introduction

Every business is the result of its owner's beliefs. Many of these beliefs are correct and can bring great profits. but that it's not always the case. In fact, when I do the preliminary analysis of a new business that wants to work with my marketing agency, I come to face the many limiting beliefs that the owner passes on to his company. It is the owner's beliefs that are reflected in his business choices and consequently in the results of the business itself.

Even marketing problems almost always come from these beliefs, and years of work and experience in the industry have shown me that these mistaken beliefs are more or less the same for everybody. They are the cause of bad business habits and therefore the reason for a less than thriving business or, more often, a business in a critical situation.

There are many aspects of a business that could very easily be improved to generate a big economic impact. I'm talking about significant benefits and improvements with minimal effort and change.

Let's take a look at some of the most common mental barriers I have faced over the years in this business. Then throughout the book, we'll address how to overcome these mental barriers to see more customers walk through the door of our store whether it's physical or virtual, and we'll look at how to hold on to these customers tightly without ceding them to the competition.

Many business owners think that they are the only ones who know how to do something in their company, that their method is the only viable one, and, in doing so, they end up overworked. These owners focus on the practical work, and how much care they put into it, and are convinced that no one else can do the same thing as well as they do it.

It is also a common belief of these business owners that customers must come to them on their own because it has always been that way in the past and it must continue to be that way in the future as if the market is static and unchanging.

They believe that if their product is good, there is no need for advertising or marketing. They believe that it is not necessary to be able to sell because if a product is good it will sell itself.

Another group of beliefs that these business owners share and that has a fundamental impact on the economics of the business regards the care of their long-term customers, those people who recurrently buy from them, and have always done so.

The common idea is that these people have always bought from them and therefore will always continue to do so. They think that there is no need to feel grateful for their loyalty in buying as if that loyalty is owed to them. They value these important customers in the same way as a casual shopper who is buying from them for the first time.

I could go on and on with many other misconceptions that if rectified can bring significant improvements to a business. The ones listed are the most prevalent and damaging, and in this book, I will reveal what aspects to check to avoid running into these erroneous beliefs, and what to do on a practical level to control the damage caused by them to improve the health of your business and the revenue it generates.

Over the next few chapters, I will cover all of the above topics and many more that will be extremely helpful to you. You will also find many practical tips that you can apply right away to see immediate improvements in your business.

Enjoy your reading!

Chapter 1

Improving Your Mindset to Improve Your Business

Owning a business is very challenging!

You have to manage a lot of things and you're busy all day long. Even when you're not physically in the company you keep thinking about it, you go to bed at night and wake up in the morning already having in your head what you have to do: appointments, deadlines, payments, meetings, ...

In this book, I want to address with you some aspects that can improve your business, starting from the most important person, which is you! We'll talk about the best way to use some proven methods to improve your work life and your business profits.

Surely right now you're implementing some sort of strategies for your business that are bringing you results you like. There are also aspects that you surely want to improve because you don't like the way they are now. Maybe you want to find new solutions, you want to have new points of view to work on, and maybe even increase the revenue of your business.

It is great to have a business that we like and to do the work that we have chosen, but sometimes the earnings do not keep up with the expectations that we have created or have decreased over time. If the economic situation of your business is difficult or you simply want to earn more money than you're making now, you need to start making improvements. You can't keep doing the same things and hoping to get different results.

In the next few chapters, I'll give you some ideas on what improvements to make in your business to bring earnings back to what they were, or up to your expectations. You may already be applying some solutions, but on the following pages, you'll find new insights and new ideas to improve them even more. I will show you exactly the same actions I take with the business owners that decide to follow a path of growth with my company.

There are so many people who walk into their business every day and wait for the sales to come on their own. Other people look for ways to sell their products without success because they don't understand where the problem lies. This is your starting point to change things.

The first topic we're going to address is Mindset, which is the mindset of both the man and the entrepreneur behind that man.

With the term "mindset", I mean all those wrong beliefs of the entrepreneur described above, and all the negative thoughts described that harm the business. To improve, change, and get new results you have to have the right mindset. If there is a problem in the business, the cause is a mistaken belief of the entrepreneur who runs it. It's a hard reality to swallow, but accepting it is the first step to success. In the next few pages, I'll show you how the right mindset can allow you to live a better life, and I'll explain how it's possible to change your point of view constructively and permanently for a future full of results that meet your expectations.

Once a correct entrepreneurial mindset is in place, it will be easy for you to see which aspects I will show you that need to be improved within your business in order to have different and better results than the current ones.

Don't take lightly the part about mindset because it is the most important part and the one that will make the difference in the results you will achieve, now, and in the future. You are probably applying solutions of some kind right now, but if your mindset is based on wrong beliefs or beliefs that are dysfunctional to your success, you are either not applying them correctly or you are not applying the right ones for your circumstances. This is because the wrong beliefs make you see things in the wrong way and the desired results won't come.

To choose the topics to cover in this book, I considered those that my experience has shown me to be the most important and controversial in the transformation to a successful business mindset that then leads to finding new winning solutions.

I have taken care to highlight everything that, in my opinion, needs to be analyzed, modified, changed, and transformed to develop a successful business mindset.

What you will find in this book is not the result of theory without foundation. As I told you before, in this book I bring you my solutions. I have applied them personally, I apply them in my companies, and I bind them to my clients and their companies to change their results for the better.

Chapter 2

First Steps

To have a business that works well, it has to work at its best even if the owner is not always there.

If you have a business, you will always have many aspects of it to take care of so that it improves.

These aspects can be: managing the staff, taking care of the production, taking care of the acquisition of new customers, maintaining the relationship with the old ones, following the marketing, taking care of the sales, analyzing and controlling the financial situation, taking care of the personal improvement to create new things... and this just to name the main ones.

I, as the owner, have to take care of all these aspects, but if I have to take direct care of all these things myself, in a short time I will run out of resources, and leave some fundamental aspects behind. It's normal, no one has infinite energy and infinite time. If I want to grow my business I can't afford to have key areas that get out of control. The only way to avoid this is to start delegating. Delegation is the first and most fearsome mindset obstacle that many entrepreneurs face. Remember in the introduction when we talked about those business owners who believe that no one can do things better than they can? This mistaken belief of theirs prevents them from making good and constructive use of delegation.

Delegating doesn't mean totally forgetting about a particular thing. It means gradually teaching someone how to do the task, with constant supervision, which is less time-consuming than doing it fully, and well.

Not everything needs to be delegated. The entrepreneur's skill lies in understanding which areas are best to delegate because they have less impact on the economic side, so to free up time for those areas that really make a difference. The entrepreneur's main job is to make sure his company makes money.

To avoid ending up in a critical situation (or to get out of it if you already are in) you must, first, know which areas are key to your business. Which ones are the areas you need to take care of to make a difference, and which ones you can delegate?

Anyone who has a business that works well understands immediately what are the key areas that must always take care of personally to bring the business into profit. In fact, the entrepreneur's first responsibility to his or her business is to implement the strategies necessary to turn the business into a profit. Once the owner has succeeded in turning the business into a profit, he or she can evaluate strategies to improve it, and others to maintain that profit over time.

When I started my first business I found myself literally swamped with a lot of things to do. I had to change that because there was no way I could do it all on my own.

I found experts I studied with who taught me that to improve my situation I had to understand what my tasks were within the company, and which ones were critically important that I had to do myself because they were too important to be delegated.

This action easily showed me which activities I could delegate. Applying these strategies, my situation improved dramatically in a short time. My mindset had changed, I had understood the fundamental role of delegation for the entrepreneur, which ones were the important things that I had to do, and which ones others had to do to make my company work well.

This new way of looking at things and doing things made my business revenue grow significantly and the fact that my business was running better also greatly improved the quality of my life.

I meet so many people daily who want to improve their results. Most of them cannot see a way to change their unsatisfactory results because of the way they think. They try a little bit and then they give up. Only the most tenacious ones continue to look for a solution to their problems and work on them. This is also a mentality matter, they have the belief that they will never give up, always keep going, and see it through. The not-so-tenacious ones who understand that it is only a matter of belief, slowly succeed. All of them manage to achieve enormous improvements and surprising results. Those who persist in not working on their mindset will not advance an inch and they won't even stay where they are. They will fall further and further down because those who don't get better get worse, it's impossible to stay still in life.

The right mindset and the right strategy make it possible for these tenacious people to achieve results that for most people seem unthinkable. In the next chapters, we will address the mindset and strategy of these successful entrepreneurs.

Chapter 3

The Courage to Change

When I first talk about my method, some people think it can't work for them.

They are convinced that improving their mindset to improve their business and what it produces, as a result, is something beyond their reach. When I point out to them that dealing with getting new clients and managing existing ones should be their priority, they think they don't have the time to deal with it because they're busy enough with everything else they already do.

They are right and I understand their point! That's why it's critical to work on your idea of delegation and create time for the tasks that really matter. Customers are a fundamental aspect of any business and they must be taken care of carefully. You must find ways to give them the attention they deserve.

The response of some skeptics to this scarcity of time for important things is to pretend that it is a normal circumstance and so they hope that things will go on by themselves in the best way possible because it worked in the past. These people think that one way or another the solution to their problems will come by itself, as if by magic. The truth is that hope is always a lame strategy.

The skeptics' excuses don't end there. They tell themselves that they are not capable of it, or that they have heard that these methods are expensive and do not work for everyone, obviously without any real, direct, and actual proof.

The only thought of this category of businessmen is to go to the store, raise the shutter, and hope customers will magically appear through the door, without any previous work that is a valid reason for this to happen. Only acting in the right direction could motivate their hope. They've probably always done this way and they don't care that conditions are constantly changing because their mindset is based on these old beliefs. The truth is that everything around the business world is constantly changing at an ever-increasing rate. For example, customers, their age group, and even their purchasing methods change at a very fast pace.

Even those who are doing well now must know that it won't last forever, business always has ups and downs. I don't say this to wish ill. Those who have had a business for years know very well that even if the business is doing well today you still have to keep working on improving it to keep up with the time changes. If you don't do constant work in this sense sales, inevitably, will drop.

Another behavior dictated by a failure-oriented mindset that I often come up against is the idea that it takes too much money to improve a situation so it is better to leave things as they are. The interesting thing about this attitude is that it is done a priori, without knowing the costs, without doing the math, and without analyzing the situation. Business owners that share these ideas live in the world of illusions, hoping for better times that never come because they do not act in any new way towards the results they wish to accomplish. I repeat what I already mentioned before, it is impossible to get different results by doing the same things, and believing the contrary is the same as believing in fairy tales.

I think that the money you spend to improve your business is relative if there is an adequate economic return. It is indeed impossible to scientifically predict the return on money invested in your business, otherwise being an entrepreneur would be a much easier job. It is also true that those who start with the idea that it is not possible to make a return on marketing investment for their business exclude a priori many important opportunities for improvement and profit growth.

In my opinion, the main problem behind all these attitudes and misconceptions is change. Change is difficult, especially if you have always worked in a certain way. Changing your habits is difficult in any area of life and the field of business is no exception. Adopting new ways of working, figuring out how to better manage clients, how to acquire new clients, etc. becomes very difficult and sometimes scary. Plus, change requires a major commitment that not everyone feels like making.

If you who are reading this have your own business, if you have a management system in your business that you started a long time ago, it doesn't necessarily mean that things are going well now or that they couldn't be even better. Think about it honestly and don't hide behind unnecessary excuses. Don't tell yourself that everything is fine because you've always done it this way, that the way you do it is right, and even though many others have better results, you can't do more than that because your business is different. Don't hide behind a thousand excuses disguised as insurmountable problems.

Focus on the idea that to have different results you have to do different things and stimulate your mind with new thoughts and circumstances so that you get different ideas. To stimulate your mind and have different ideas you have to accept change.

The most difficult factor to deal with in facing any change is fear. Fear fades away if you have courage, that same courage that you used to do something that many people don't want to do, the courage you showed when you decided to open up your Business.

There is a very useful saying that goes: "One day fear knocked on the door, courage went to open it, and found no one".

To improve your business you have to use your courage to change your mindset, which will change your actions, which will change your results.

Chapter 4
Analyze What You Do

I've had several businesses that I didn't know anything about at first and I thought all I had to do was listen, understand, and copy what others were doing to make things go well.

I thought that being told what to do without any understanding was enough. As long as somebody would tell me what to do and how to do it, I thought everything would just be fine and the money would come to me on its own.

All around me I saw loads of people working non-stop all day, struggling with a thousand things. They were taking care of everything and they would tell me, "I have to do everything myself because nobody does things the way I do." It was one of my first experiences so I thought it was true. I could see them slaving away all day and working on a thousand different things all the time.

It didn't take long to realize that the reality was very different. He had to do it all because he wasn't willing to delegate even the smallest task for fear of losing control. Many could have done a better job, but they were not allowed to try to do it, the owner was always in fear of losing his role and being belittled. Many of the activities performed during each day were totally unnecessary, but by doing everything on your own it becomes difficult to question an inadequate method. Finally, in the long run, the energies run out and you end up making a big mess.

I have done different jobs and owned businesses in different areas, and my clients come from different categories of business. This has led me to understand some fundamental things. One of my most important discoveries is that for every problem there is already a solution or even more than one, even when we can't see it yet. Another fundamental thing I realized is that a person coming from another field can help me find the solution for an issue that is not in their competence because they see things from a different point of view, not conditioned by the beliefs related to that specific field.

At the beginning of my entrepreneurial experience I thought that the more I worked and did "things", the more money I would make. "Work hard and the results will come." That's what I was told, that's what I saw every day, and that's what my beliefs were based on.

Doing different jobs and having businesses in different areas made me realize that what people around me were telling me didn't work. I found myself in situations were working harder was not enough and others where working harder was not even possible. It wasn't enough for me to work harder to make things better, because no matter what, my efforts didn't change anything.

I had been led to believe that time spent reading and studying was useless, that I needed to do more "stuff", I just needed to put more effort into what I was already doing, and the results would come. Meeting new people and different approaches to problem-solving made me reconsider, reflect, and opened up to a new way of thinking and doing. I saw things in a totally different and new way. I gained a new amazing perspective and that made a huge change in me, in my working life, and in my business. First of all, I realized that doing more of the same things that are giving me undesirable results would only give me more undesirable results. Next, I understood that I couldn't do it alone, I needed 2 categories of people. I needed people who were able to help me, people to whom I could delegate, and hands-on help in accomplishing certain tasks so that I could be free to focus only on the tasks of greatest importance.

I also needed people who could help me understand new and different subjects and approaches. I needed to learn about new and different ways of thinking. I began to understand the importance of studying people who had already achieved the results I wanted, and who had knowledge that I could apply and replicate to get the results I wanted.

With my study and the advice of these people, I changed my methods of approach and execution in many areas. I changed my mindset and with it the health of my business and my financial situation.

I started to delegate the most unimportant tasks and focus all my attention only on the really important ones that made a difference for my business. At that point, my results started to change.

One aspect on which I focused a lot was to find those who could help me in two aspects that I consider fundamental for every business. I'm talking about finding new customers and improving the relationship with the existing ones.

When I found myself with some big business problems, I realized that everything I previously thought was important really wasn't important at all. Thanks to the new way of looking at things I was developing and the new ideas that sparked from my new way of thinking, I was able to apply new, better strategies, and I was able to get through the tough times and solve my problems.

Thanks to these important lessons learned in the past, I still continue to search for new strategies, new approaches, and new solutions for this ever-changing market.

The purpose of this book is to take you on a journey of understanding the importance of mindset, change to get new results, and develop new winning strategies that you can apply to reach full entrepreneurial success.

Chapter 5

When You Can't Stay in Business

A few years ago, almost overnight, I found myself in the situation of no longer being able to welcome my usual type of customers in my businesses, for various reasons which I won't go into detail about. I had expenses to pay of course, but I couldn't earn money!

This type of circumstance in business is quite frequent, perhaps not in a situation like mine, but with a very similar basic criterion.

I'm referring to those activities that are blocked or whose flow of customers decreases, for a series of problems beyond their control. I'll give you a few examples to explain myself better. Sometimes you see restaurants on busy streets. They have easy access to the road, a good parking lot, and various favorable conditions related to high traffic and proximity to the road. One fine day, due to a road renovation, the direct access to the restaurant gets removed. Where there used to be direct access to the parking lot, there is now a guardrail blocking the road. The access is no longer so simple and direct for those traveling on the busy road. Those who want to stop and eat have to make a very long turn to get around the obstacle. As the favorable circumstance changes, the desire to stop there to eat passes, and it results in the loss of many customers.

Think of a business built near a busy highway exit. For reasons of maintenance of the highway, the tollbooth is closed for a long period, the flow of traffic immediately decreases a lot, and with it also the income of the commercial activity that benefited from it.

How many times have you seen or heard these things happen? And if you're now telling yourself that you don't care because you have an online business, you're dead wrong. This argument applies to an online business as well. Imagine what happens to an online business that gets all its customers and traffic from advertisements made on a certain platform. What happens if the platform gets shut down or blocks your ability to advertise? The same as our physical businesses, which is the loss of a lot of customers.

Many reasons can lead to such circumstances and they are also very common. I am reminded of a business owner in my area that I spoke with recently. In his area, he was the leader in selling a range of products for which he had no competitors. When the competition arrived and entered the market with lower prices, they took away his customers, and his business closed down.

Indeed, those who charge low prices cannot stay in business for long. It is also true that there are plenty of people who can take the place of the competition and try in turn to overtake the Leader.

Many people have money to throw away and who, even though they don't know how to do business, can go and bother a business that had always worked well before.

When one closes, there is immediately another ready to take its place. And what does the Leader do? If he doesn't change his strategies and his way of doing business, he resists until he has the money and then, inevitably, he succumbs.

It is difficult, if not impossible, to have a business that works if you are not aware of all the circumstances that can change and the facts that can happen.

I know this well, both because I've experienced it all firsthand and because I work with people who have problems like this to help them find useful solutions.

These are real problems that can happen and indeed do happen often. Coming out of them is difficult if you don't know how to do it. Later in the book, we'll see why the right mindset can help you overcome or avoid these kinds of difficult situations.

Chapter 6

I Was Missing an Important Piece

As I mentioned at the beginning of the previous chapter, my situation was not good. Nor is it good for all the people who have a business, to have to fight for it every day because they are slowed down, and encounter continuous obstacles. Their business is their passion, it feeds their family, and it is their source of income, so it is normal to want to fight to overcome obstacles.

In looking for a solution to my problem, I have met so many different people. I met people who had businesses that worked, people who made good money, and people who were very well educated such as professors and luminaries in their field. I would talk to them, but what they were telling me didn't work for my situation. Where was the problem?

As I mentioned earlier, you struggle in every way to overcome obstacles, so I kept striving in continuous search for solutions. I started talking to people from all walks of life about my work, and my business problems, and I was doing it to seek comparison. One day I met a guy named Mattia. He was an advertising graphic designer, his job was to graphically design business cards, flyers, and similar advertising products.

When I exposed my problem to him, he responded by asking me a question. On the surface, that question might have seemed very obvious but for me and for my mindset at the time, clearly, it was not.

He asked me, "How do you reach out to people to let them know about your business?"

Mattia wasn't directly involved in Marketing, Advertising, and Sales but, because of his job, he was constantly in close contact with people in that area all day long. He would graphically implement what customers wanted to show about their businesses.

I never had a problem with reaching people because they always came to me spontaneously without me doing anything. But now I need a new group of customers, I couldn't let in the previous category, and so I definitely needed to let people know about my business. I had no skill in this area and my mindset had never even allowed me to see the need to develop such a skill.

That simple question made me realize that at that precise moment the rules for my business had changed and I had to change my approach (mindset) because the old way didn't and couldn't work anymore.

What amazed me the most was the fact that out of all the people I had talked to who had a business, no one had thought to direct me towards this kind of topic so that I could change my approach to my business.

Obviously, after that chat with Mattia, whom I thanked profusely, a new world opened up to me. I could reorganize my business to target a different audience than the ones that had been my regular customers up to that moment. To do that I just had to put in place precise strategies that would allow me to reach exactly those people. The first and most important step was to change my mindset about business dynamics. With a new mindset, I could find new ways to do things and solve the problem.

I immediately went looking for people who could help me. I looked for and found people who had the information that would allow me to do the new things that needed to be done. Then I studied and applied that information. Finally, I implemented a series of strategies that allowed me to get the new results I wanted.

Chapter 7

Finding the Right Solutions

Almost always, the obstacles that don't allow us to get the results we want we've created ourselves.

What does that mean? It means that if you talk to a person who has a business that works well and that makes millions, he won't tell you what's not working unless you ask them directly. That kind of person will talk to you about the solutions he applied to get where he is now, he'll talk to you about those things that made the difference for him, and it doesn't occur to you to contradict him because he's got the results, he's done it, he's figured it out, and he's applied it, so he has experience.

Surely, if you're smart, you'll treasure what he's told you, then you'll go from there to find new ways.

On the other hand, if you talk to a person who has an unsuccessful business, he will immediately put the problems in front of you because his mind is focused on that, on the problems, and not on the solutions. That's the problem! You go where your focus is. If you focus on problems, you will get into trouble. If you focus on solutions, you go towards success and satisfaction.

This problem-oriented mindset is exactly what is preventing them from succeeding. This kind of entrepreneur keeps focusing only on problems, he tells himself that he already knows what he needs to know, and he doesn't need to learn anything new. Unfortunately, with this mentality, he can't go anywhere and when you try to reason with him about this he finds other excuses.

Maybe he realizes that he needs to change something, he tries hard, but he doesn't get the desired results right away, so he quits.

Results don't come overnight. They are the result of commitment, study, work, and the right mindset. If you have to apply something you've never done, it takes a lapse of time to make it work because you'll make mistakes, that's normal, nothing usually goes right the first time.

Sometimes realizing that there are criticalities in what needs to be done stops people and makes them give up before they even start.

Instead, the solution is found by insisting, trying, trying again, and continuing on that path. You can't change your path every time you face an obstacle. Obstacles will always be there, even more so if for 10 or 20 years you've been working in a certain way, and now the rules change. You have to adapt to the changes and you have to give yourself time to make the solution work for you.

I see too many business owners quit when they have to implement a new way of working. They quit because it takes new skills or because they have to take time away from their hobbies to spend more time on the new method. They quit and go back to their work comfort zone because they feel safe there. In truth, things are not safe at all in that work comfort zone. The fact that they have been doing the same things for so long gives them a sense of security through habit, making them feel safe in their minds even if this is not the case at all.

All it takes is a small period of crisis, maybe a phase of change, and all their security collapses like a small sandcastle washed by a wave.

There is a segment of businessmen who are too afraid to face reality. This category of people prefers to put their heads under the sand. They see that things are not going well, they see that they absolutely must change something, but their head tells them something else. As always, it is the mindset that drives the actions.

These entrepreneurs hope that someday things will change to go back to the way they were before the crisis or market change. They wait, they hope, and they tell themselves "I have to wait just a little longer". In that static wait, they let everything slip through their fingers until they find themselves without customers.

Hope is important, but it must have a concrete basis. Hope just for the sake of hoping is useless. Hope must be based on massive doses of concrete action so that things can change for the better.

I can't walk into my store and hope that customers are coming in by sheer luck. I can't justify myself with the fact that I've always done it this way, that things have always been this way, that sooner or later the customers will come back. They won't come back unless you take action to make them come back.

Some people justify themselves by saying, "I take concrete actions to attract customers! I advertise on billboards!". Think about it. In a car, a driver drives past a billboard at least 40 to 60 miles per hour. The billboard usually shows the name of the business, the address of where it is located, what it does, maybe some of the products it sells, the phone number, any discounts, and maybe it even shows "Timmy the Otter" the mascot of the business.

Come on, let's be serious! Do you really think someone passing by at that speed can read anything on your billboard? Do you really think a driver can take his attention away from driving for more than a handful of seconds? Do you think he can afford to read the whole sign? Do you think that while he's driving his attention isn't a million light-years away from your sign? If he even notices your billboard and manages to read something, what are the chances that he will be on target with your product or service? What are the chances that the person paying attention could be your potential customer?

The actions that need to be taken are quite different. It takes study, commitment, and time to plan specific and targeted activities that can lead your business to improve and have more customers.

Some companies are now doing well, doing all the right things, and having their own program to follow that has always brought them the desired results.

What has been said so far applies to them as well. Things are not sure, because the rule is valid for everyone: everything is constantly changing! If those companies want to remain at the top where they are now, they too must constantly seek out and apply new strategies. They don't have the luxury of remaining static and stationary unless they want to lose their place at the top.

If competitors were to come along (and sooner or later it happens), current strategies would no longer be useful because they would have to change their approach to the entire market. A new competitor, by necessity, changes the rules.

You have to adapt, you have to change, and you have to revise what you have always been doing up to adapt it to the new needs. So, no one that owns a business can sit comfortably. Whoever wishes to be comfortable should never start a business.

Anyone who says to have a business and he can sit comfortably, is either not making any money, he will soon stop making money, or he is on his way to closing down.

I don't mean this in a bad way. I talk to a lot of people who have businesses that work and make good money, and not one of them has ever used the word "comfortable". They use other words to define their business. They call it "beautiful", "exciting", and "satisfying", but no one ever tells me they live a "quiet" and "comfortable" business life. It is a condition that many business owners would like to have but unfortunately, it is an unattainable condition. There always is work to be done and things to take care of.

Chapter 8

Let's Take Action with My 5-Steps Method

Part 1: You

In the previous chapters, I went into a bit of detail about the problems of business owners, how they are related to the mindset of the entrepreneur behind that business, and also how often a certain mindset prevents you from seeing the problem. All we have seen so far helped me to introduce you to the topics we're going to discuss and work on from here on out. It also helped me to get you to identify yourself in some of the scenarios described so that you can make a better profit from what you are going to read in the following pages. You may have identified with one of the mindset issues, or your business may have taken a hit due to the unfortunate events that have occurred over the last two and a half years, and you may have identified with that circumstance. Let's take a practical look at what you can do to make your business truly successful.

In this chapter, I'll explain which are the most important characteristics of a successful business. I will list the 5 factors that I believe should be taken into account to change your actions and, consequently, change and improve your business.

The first part of my method includes 3 steps. Each of these steps regards some kind of work you have to do on yourself. We will analyze your mindset, your routine, and your actions. Once you've got those basics in place, we'll move on to part two. Part two includes the two final steps of my method. The two critical business factors that you'll need to address in a new way, thanks to the work you've done on yourself in part one. I'm referring to acquiring and retaining your customers.

Let's get started!

Step 1: Mindset

As we have mentioned at various points in previous chapters, the starting point for the entire improvement process is the mentality of the entrepreneur, his mindset as it is often called nowadays. You have to move from a scarcity and failure mindset to a success mindset.

What happens to most business owners is that they don't have the right beliefs to get the desired results.

When we tackle something new a thousand thoughts are running through our heads, many fears, and just as many uncertainties.

When I work with a new client who is hampered by a fear of the outcomes of bringing something new to the business, I have him think back to when he had just opened. At that time everything was new and all outcomes were uncertain, just as they are now if he were to do something new.

Despite all the thoughts of uncertainty at the time of starting the business he did it anyway and slowly adjusted his pitch to get results.

At this point, usually, the owner in question will object to me that he now has a lot more to lose if he makes mistakes. Now he somehow floats and the business survives but a mistake at this stage could be fatal.

The entrepreneur doesn't always realize that he has a lot to lose by simply floating and getting by. All it takes is a small, unexpected, and unlikely change to wipe out everything in a second. I think a lot of them learned the lesson the hard way during the pandemic and the period of the various lockdowns.

So, to improve a business you need to strengthen your mindset, your psychology, and your beliefs. To do this I personally study a lot. I carve out a few hours a day to delve into the topics that interest and serve me.

This allows me to always have new ideas and apply what I study to improve my work.

For example, I read a lot of biographies of entrepreneurs who have been very successful in various business fields.

This serves on a subconscious level to tell my head, "Look at these people! They've been successful. Despite the adversity they made it!"

This is a very important element. On a conscious level, we realize that there are people who make it. (Or at least I hope that's the case, otherwise, I suggest you change your surroundings immediately and go where there are serious people, working, and making lots of money.)

Even if on a conscious level we tell ourselves that it is possible to make it, because of our past conditioning on a subconscious level we may not really believe it. Without a true deep belief that we can do it, we don't put in the right amount of effort, and end up frustrated. Reading so many success stories helps you gradually gain the subconscious belief that you can do it without a shadow of a doubt.

Another thing I try to do as much as possible is to be with people who achieve the results I want to achieve.

The reason I do this is pretty simple. Have you ever heard the phrase, "We are the result of the people we hang out with"? I guess you have. The truth of that phrase is that if one is hanging out with four jerks who don't make a dime, he is definitely the fifth.

If the people you hang out with earn 1,000$, you will probably earn 1,000$ yourself.

My advice is to look for a better environment where you can hang out with people who already earn the money you would like to earn, who have a successful business with the characteristics you would like to have in yours, and live an entrepreneurial life like the one you would like. You'll see the world from a new and winning perspective, and you'll start getting new ideas to apply to your business.

Another helpful thing you can do is condition your mind to the results you want to achieve.

I have written a book on this subject, which explains how to do this through the use of Visualization techniques.

It's titled "The Power Of Visualization - How Successful People Use the Power of the Mind to Achieve Goals and Get Everything They Want in Personal Life and Business" by Azione Business.

Look it up and read it, it's sure to give you new insights. If you've never done so, start putting into practice my advice you'll find inside it and you'll benefit from it immediately.

Basically, the principle I explain in that book is based on exploiting the brain's ability to take for granted everything we imagine, even if it is not real.

I'll just give you a quick explanation of how it works since it is treated in depth in the book. I truly encourage you to read the full method in the book because the techniques explained can make a huge difference in your life and in your business.

If we imagine in detail in our mind the result we want to achieve as if it were a kind of mental film full of details and we continue to repeat these images in our mind, our mind in turn will do a whole series of processes that will lead us to change all our results.

Obviously, to work properly, this whole process must be followed by concrete and practical actions, but those actions will come spontaneously because the repetition done through the visualization process will reprogram your subconscious mind which controls most of your actions.

For example, if I want to improve my sales process, i.e. sell my products to someone, I would start by first living the sales experience in my mind. I would do this through mental imagery where I would see all of the sequences of that sale, visualizing all of the steps, all of the customer's objections, if any, and my attitude during the process. With repeated practice of this visualization, I can improve one by one all the aspects visualized. When the moment of a real sale comes, I will feel different, more comfortable, and more confident because I have already lived that experience so many times in my mind (and the mind makes no distinction between real and imaginary, remember) and so I will have a result I never had before. Nothing will change if you just exercise but the moment you will go to see a customer and start your selling presentation you will get huge tangible results. As an entrepreneur, create a nice mental movie about your ideal company, its processes, its results, your life as a successful entrepreneur, the emotions related to this new condition, and so on. Repeat the mental movie daily and act accordingly. This practice will give you new ideas, and faith in the results, and help you develop your new entrepreneurial mindset.

Summarizing this section, we can say that a key part to improve in business is to develop a new success-oriented mindset based on the belief that you can be as successful as you want to be and have faith in this belief.

Step 2: Routine

What is a "Routine"? Routine is the method, in sequence, that we use to do a job or, in general, to do anything.

To put it in different words, the time I wake up every day, the number of hours I dedicate to work, the hours I dedicate to my family, etc. form my routine.

Having a routine is very useful because it allows us to organize our day to perform at our best in everything we do.

We all possess mental energy that is limited and is not always at the same value. At certain times and circumstances, it works better, sometimes we waste it unnecessarily, and feel tired before we even start doing anything.

I've learned to use this method of creating a routine and seeing things accordingly through training at the gym.

When you dedicate an hour to physical training, there are many factors to consider.

If all of these factors are not organized properly, they take away valuable resources.

I work out every day, and the fact that I follow a studied pattern of sequenced movements (a routine) is very helpful and keeps me from wasting valuable resources (i.e., time and energy).

The very fact of organizing myself so that I have an hour a day to train is part of a sequence of my routine.

This kind of organization comes from the need not to waste my time.

Time is a very important resource, in fact, I would say it is the most important of all even more important than money.

You cannot have more time than others. We all have the same time and using it in the best possible way is fundamental for those who have a goal to achieve.

Imagine if you were to go to the gym and start thinking about what kind of workout to do, how to do it, what it takes to do it, and so on. You would spend the hour at your disposal without having accomplished anything. Instead, having a studied pattern of sequenced movements like mine allows you to make the most of this hour.

There is another important aspect to consider when using routines: I can have a routine within a routine.

What do I mean by that? The fact that I have a specific time set to workout makes me focus on what I'm doing. I know that during the day I have several blocks of time, each dedicated to a specific task.

I have a series of blocks of time, organized in a certain way. Those blocks of time make up my routine.

Each of these blocks in turn can be organized into other organized sub-blocks that form a routine in the day's routine.

I'll use the training example again to explain more clearly. We said that I have a block of time, let's say an hour, and in this hour I can choose to do different exercises. If I train in martial arts, I can devote 20 minutes to endurance, 20 minutes to speed, and the last 20 minutes of the hour to stretching.

With this ready-made pattern, I don't have to waste mental energy thinking about what I might do, and during my hour of training, I have total mental energy dedicated to getting the most out of my workout. I can perform at my best because I have no distracting thoughts and, in this way, I can continuously improve my performance. After my workout, I will go to my office because the second daily block of my routine involves me working on my new book for a two-hour block. That two-hour block will in turn be organized into a precise sub-routine so that I waste neither a precious minute nor my energy.

This concept of routines and sub-routines is critically important for work and productivity. For example, to successfully write this book, I had to schedule its writing within my daily routine.

I devoted two hours a day to writing this book. To do this, I selected the time of day when I am most productive to best accomplish this task, then drafted, and followed a structured writing schedule. Another important choice I urge you to make to get the most out of each of your important daily activities is to figure out what your best and most productive time is for each activity.

This reminds me of a piece of advice I gave to a friend of mine, after a "chat" about personal productivity, that might be useful to you as well.

My friend was complaining that he couldn't focus on his work because he had too much distracting interference at home.

I asked him a couple of questions to find out what his daily routine was (unknowingly because he had never voluntarily organized one) and advised him to wake up in the morning two or three hours before the rest of the family so that he could focus on his work in total peace for those two or three hours. He did so, and after a short time, he contacted me to thank me for the huge increase and improvement in productivity that occurred as a result of this simple action.

Waking up before everyone else has, mainly, two very positive aspects. The first aspect is practical, in fact, you can benefit from silence and tranquility which are the ideal conditions for concentration and productivity. The second aspect is motivation. Waking up before everyone else allows you to win before everyone else. You are awake while others are asleep. Just getting up early, before everyone else puts me in a positive state of winning.

Going back to productivity, find your best time (for you it may not be very early in the morning, although for many it is), the one where you are most productive, and organize yourself so that you can devote that time to the activities of greatest importance.

For example, dedicating an hour a day every day to creating new material for your new project will certainly improve its success and your path to your goal.

If that hour is always at the same time each day, you will save yourself a lot of mental energy. You will save mental energy because you won't have to think: "What do I do now?". This allows you to be as focused as possible on what you're doing and having more focus on what you're doing equals better results.

Have you ever seen those people who always dress the same way? Dressing the same way all the time is a method for saving mental energy. So much energy is wasted in deciding what clothes to put on each day. Dressing always the same allows this important energy saved to be used in a better way in other moments.

My suggestion is to organize your day with a routine of useful actions that you will perform mechanically and organize each action with a sub-routine.

You have to look for the best sequence for you. To do this you will need to try various combinations of actions, various sequences of exercises, and different times of the day for each trial.

If you don't already have a routine to perfect, I suggest you make a list of all the tasks you do during a day in the order you do them. Take a look to see if there are any unnecessary actions that you can replace with something better. For example, if you read the newspaper every morning, stop, and read a book useful for your growth instead. On your list are television, video games, checking your personal profile on social media, and hours and hours of consulting emails? I'm sure you can find more useful and constructive actions to replace these. Once you've drawn up a sequence, try gradually changing part of that sequence by moving various tasks to different times in your day, and take note if doing them at different times gets you better results.

Remember the case of my friend I mentioned earlier? Doing some tasks in those two quiet hours early in the morning where he can focus on his work with more concentration has benefited him enormously. You may discover a similar and simple solution for yourself as well.

My advice, then, is to build and have a well-structured routine, a sequence to follow, and repeat every day to constantly improve what you do.

This will help you even and especially on the less favorable days. There are bound to be days when you want to rest and do nothing. When you repeat daily actions mechanically thanks to the routine, you'll find it easier to do it even on those tough days when you don't feel like it.

My workout routine, for example, makes me work out even on days when I'm not very fit. My productivity routine for writing a book, planning a marketing campaign, or studying and improving my tasks allows me to be productive even on the days when I'm laziest.

Give it a try yourself! Put down a sequence of things you want to do and stick with it for a few days. Then change it up, put in, take out, and add what feels best for you. Build a path to find your ideal daily routine.

The important thing is to do it and you'll see that you'll start to see the first signs of improvement right away.

Step 3: Act

It is acting that allows us to have the results we want, that allows us to achieve our goals. It is through action that we achieve success.

Often people do not understand that action is the solution they are looking for.

Doing and acting are two very important concepts that need to be clarified and understood.

I introduced this topic because I find that it is critical to understand the concept of doing and acting.

In many books I have read, I find that the fundamental concept of the need to act is never stressed enough. I can think of many marketing and sales books that I have studied over the years. In these books, it seems that on a logical level everything runs smoothly. You, the reader, take what the author explains at face value. Then, perhaps, you want to put into practice what you have read and you realize that it is not possible because there is something that does not work. You try many times without success.

You justify yourself by thinking that maybe you are not applying it correctly.

Instead, I have studied other books on the same topics that at a logical level might seem difficult and counterintuitive, but once you apply the rules described, they work immediately.

This makes me think that many authors have never personally applied what they teach, they just lay out a theory and because of this they probably don't put enough focus on the role of action. To improve the fortunes of your business, another important mental switch you'll have to make is to get used to the fact that doing and applying what you study makes all the difference. This book is a great tool and is entirely based on proven practice, the kind I practice and apply myself to help my clients' businesses grow. But you have to put into practice what you read, it is the only way to get results. Just reading it won't be enough, but you can easily apply all you are reading because it's all already Benn tested.

Even when I talk to people there is always more theory and less practice than I would like. When I visit a company and ask for an explanation of a process, "How do you do X?" I hear the reply, "That's how you do it in theory!". I am puzzled because obviously, it is the practice that counts.

I obviously don't know everything, but what I do know I know well, I know how to apply it well, and I know how to make it work great.

I am reminded of an important teaching of my Martial Arts teacher. He used to tell me that if you set up a match between two fighters where one has continuously trained chain punches for an entire year, while the other has trained 100 different techniques to look cooler, between the two of them the one who has only trained chain punches will always win. It will be less cool, but it will be absolutely effective because he became an expert in that technique.

So, you have to understand what the importance of doing and acting is. You have to get moving. It is certainly too vast a topic to be able to cover in one chapter of this book, but it is essential to introduce the concept so that you can begin to think about it.

Let's start with the basics. Where do actions come from? Actions are born from the energy we give to an idea!

This concept is very simple. When we have an idea and we work on it with our thoughts and emotions, we end up putting this idea into action.

Put another way, actions are the results of our thoughts.

When we have an irrepressible need to act, it's because we have powered up our thoughts with so much energy that we need to express that energy through action. The energy we attach to the thought can be positive or negative and this will determine the type of actions.

A thought attached to positive emotions will cause us to take positive actions.

Why am I talking about emotion? The term emotion comes from E= energy, and from motion= which stands for action, to set in motion. So, when I feel emotions there is energy in action.

When our thoughts make us feel positive emotions we will do positive actions, while when we feel negative emotions we will do negative actions.

To do better actions we need to control our thoughts.

Another element that makes us want to get moving and take action is motivation.

Again, if we analyze the word it is composed of motiv = reason and action (I don't think this one needs explaining).

So, we must also have a reason to act.

Sometimes we have the reason, while other times we don't and we have to look for it to put ourselves in action.

In a famous book on Mindset, I read about a study done on some children.

Elementary school children were sampled and taken to a room where they were seated. In front of them, on a table, was placed a lovely slice of cake or some delicious candies, as the case may be. At that point, an adult would intervene and tell them not to touch the candies or the cake. He explained that he needed to be away for a moment and that, when he returned, he would give them a prize if they did not touch the sweets on the table.

As can be imagined, most children ate the dessert immediately, but not all. Some were waiting for the adult to return. They were motivated to wait by the promise of the prize.

The scholars followed these children into adulthood. They analyzed their profession and found that children who had not touched dessert until the adult arrived had more successful careers than those who had eaten dessert immediately.

Translated into terms that may be of interest to us, what can we understand from this study?

When we do business it is our motivation that drives us to act. We perform an action to get a result in return. This result, however, is not necessarily instantaneous but may be delayed rather than immediate. Just as with the children in the test, the short-term result is smaller, while being motivated to achieve something larger requires some waiting.

Many find this concept extremely difficult because in today's society we have been accustomed to having everything right away.

This mentality creates a whole host of complications. For example, it often happens to me when talking about a business project that takes time to put into practice, that people get demotivated because they would like the desired result in a very short space of time.

Finding the right motivation and being able to postpone the reward without getting demotivated are very important qualities to develop along the road to your success. Along this road, you also need to pay close attention to blockages.

Two main elements can block us when it comes time to take action. These two elements are fear of criticism and guilt.

Fear of criticism is a fake fear. In my book on visualization, which I mentioned earlier, you will find the topic of fears very well explained, so here I will just address it more briefly and with a couple of examples.

In a seminar in Monte Carlo in the Principality of Monaco, a trainer gave me this example about fear. If a building is falling on your head you are afraid for your life, it's a real fear, and in this case, you can do one of two things, either run away towards safety or stay where you are blocked by that fear. It's a real fear because something can happen to you, you can get hurt, and you can risk your life and die.

If, on the other hand, you fear a person criticizing you for what you do, that is not a real fear. Nothing real or physical happens to you. What happens takes place entirely in your head. You make a bad mental movie about the negative consequences of those critics. It's a negative visualization and it's something that may never happen at all.

There's another important factor to consider when it comes to other people's judgment: 99% of people are wrong.

99% of people don't know what they're doing and they don't know why they're doing it. If they did, the world would be full of successful people, but it's not. 99% of people are ready to dispense useless opinions on others based on nothing.

People who criticize you probably don't even know why they're doing it themselves, how can they judge you properly? They have no chance. It's just a stupid habit that someone has taught them to replicate. If the person criticizing you would keep his mouth shut and think more about himself, he would have a much better life. Instead, because his life sucks, he has to make other people's lives suck as well by continuing to criticize them.

Now that you know that, you should stop caring about other people's opinions! Now you should be aware that those who criticize you do not have the competence to do so, they are just giving air to their vocal cords.

This is even more true for those who criticize you on social media. In your opinion, does a person who has a beautiful and healthy life have time to waste criticizing people by commenting on social media? Let's be real, anyone who does that is just a loser.

Guilt is more insidious. Many people think they don't have it or worse don't even know what it is or of its existence.

Guilt is instilled in us from a young age by parents, relatives, friends, school teachers, church, politics, and so on and becomes more and more ingrained whether fed consciously or not.

Again, this is a very broad topic and in this context, I will limit myself to dealing with it strictly for our own sake.

For the purpose of your self-improvement and your business, it may be that you don't earn as much money as you would like because in your subconscious there is a hidden belief that doing so makes you feel guilty towards those who have no money.

Reason with me for a moment. You probably get up every morning at 5 or 6 o'clock, and you spend your day between your business and studying new skills that will be useful to you. You take little vacation time and sacrifice time that you could be spending with your family to work and improve what you do. You create useful products and services, you provide solutions that others don't have, and then, somewhere inside you say to yourself, "You have to earn the right amount of money". I hope you're kidding!

Most people are already making a lot of money with their jobs. While you, who give 100% and make sacrifices, tell yourself that it is fair to earn what you are earning? That earning more would be unfair to the less fortunate?

All this is the fault of those who made you feel guilty as a kid when your subconscious was forming. It is the fault of those who instilled in you this useless and limiting belief. Obviously, it must be removed on the road to success otherwise, while you are about to take any action that can change the fate of your business, your subconscious will sabotage you and you will never take that differentiating action at all.

There is no fault in being rich and earning a lot of money, you should be proud of it!

Remember that thieves and those who steal are poor, otherwise, they wouldn't go and steal.

Those who give to charity and those who do good with their millions of dollars are rich. Those who make people feel good with their money are rich.

Don't be fooled or manipulated by those who tell you otherwise.

Part 2: Your Business

If you've carefully followed all of the first three personal steps of the business improvement process you should have figured out how to gear your business mindset toward success. Business success is measured by money. If you have been through the method in the previous chapters, you should have understood that your primary task as an entrepreneur is to make money for your business. Customers are the ones who bring money into your business, so they must become your top priority if they have not been so far.

In the last two steps of the process, we will look at specific actions that you need to take to improve the economic situation of your business. These are fundamental and decisive actions. They are also challenging actions and they require your full attention.

Remember when we first talked about delegation? Now that your entrepreneurial mindset is geared toward success, you should be able to see your business processes in a new light and delegate as much as you can. You will find yourself with time on your hands generated by delegation. You will need to use a small amount of time to check that the delegated actions are being carried out correctly, and the rest you will need to spend on the next two steps.

This does not mean that you will have to do these new things yourself. It does mean that you will need time to select the most appropriate professional to do them for you, you will need time to review their work, and you will need time to get them the materials they need to do the work for you. You'll need time to study your audience and products more closely, you'll need time to reflect, and come up with new ideas to get the most out of the next two steps, even if you don't have to put them directly into practice.

You may well decide to do this, but you should first estimate how much time you will need to study everything you need to know before you can implement the process. This time is obviously not easily estimable because it depends on your initial knowledge of the market, technology, customers, marketing, and the various channels you can use to reach people interested in your product or service.

With that said and now that your business mindset is in place, let's proceed with the process of improving your business.

Step 4: Acquire New Customers

If you own a business, customer acquisition must be your main focus.

Customer acquisition is important for the prosperity of any business. Having a flow of new customers coming through the door (even figuratively speaking) allows you to increase your earnings and live more peacefully.

Having a system that allows you to acquire customers automatically is the marketing strategy that works best.

Being able to predict how many new customers may come through your door makes you sleep better at night, allows you to make better investments, and helps you to make better decisions.

You need to constantly improve your system to acquire new customers to keep your revenue steady. You put this acquisition process into place through a well-thought-out marketing strategy.

What is Marketing? Great question!

One of the definitions I like best was given by a famous marketing expert Sergio Zyman and it goes like this: "Marketing is selling more stuff, to more people, more often, for more money, more efficiently".

So, what do you need marketing for? Marketing is a tool that helps you make more money that's why you, and every other business owner, need it.

If you have a Business this is all you need to think about and focus on.

There are several aspects you need to know to put in place all the marketing processes a business needs.

Here I will explain just a few of them, the most useful ones that you can put into practice right away. A book is not exactly the place to go into detail on such vast and important topics, but I can start to tell you about them and give you some extremely useful information.

A marketing system is one thing you absolutely must have in your business.

A system is an articulated group of elements that work together to achieve a goal.

So, having a Marketing system means having a clear understanding of what you want to achieve, having the group of elements that can lead to achieving your goal, and making sure that all the necessary elements work together in the right way to bring you success.

This process starts with your product or service and goes straight to your customers' pockets to get their money. I'm simplifying of course, because in between the starting point and the endpoint, depending on the type of business you have, there are many elements and steps to put in place and take into consideration.

Many different marketing systems can be implemented based on the result you want to achieve and the type of business you own. What you have to pay attention to, however, is that not all of them lead to your final gain. This is because, unfortunately, many people don't think it's ethical to make money in business.

I believe that making money is right and good and my teachings always start from this premise.

The main point I would like you to focus on is that you must have a method to bring customers into your business, you cannot leave it to chance.

You have to have a process, in the jargon called a "funnel," that gets people first interested in what you do, getting to know you, and knowing that you exist. Then you show them your solutions to their problem so they understand that you can help them. Once they understand you can sell them your solutions.

How do people know you? Do they know the name of your business? Do they know your face? Do they know your product? Do they know what you do?

A lot of business owners spend a lot of money to get their company name out there and show it all over the place.

There are considerations to be made about this concept, which may seem fair at first glance.

Do I really have that much money to spend to do such a massive marketing effort? Or could I invest less money with a better strategy and get better returns on my investment?

Why should people buy from me after just seeing the name of my shop?

It's very interesting to ask yourself these kinds of questions and then give yourself some answers.

What comes out of it might surprise you.

I think it's more effective to reach people through the solutions I outlined just above. First, get the word out about what you do. Then use what you do that solves a problem to bring people to you. This is much more useful than just getting your name out there.

I do this process, for example, through social media. I use social media to go get traffic, that is, to get seen by the people who make up a certain market. Then, again on social channels, I shoot images, write posts, or upload videos and I place those materials in front of these people. I make sure is stuff that attracts their attention, stimulates their interest, makes them understand what my business is all about, and how I can be their best choice. The next step is to get these people whose interest I have attracted to buy the product or service, to do it more often, and for more money.

If you analyze the last sentence carefully you will find that it contains several truths. If you don't share these truths completely you will find it difficult to make more money from your business.

Many business owners tell me that they are fine as they are. They say they don't want more money because they're already doing fine as it is.

I can say that I have owned some businesses and run others. A basic lesson I have learned from my businesses is that it is critical to have a certain mindset to grow a business and it is critical to have a different mindset to maintain those results. This is why mindset was the first step in this 5-steps method.

Even those who think they have arrived where they wanted to must work to stay where they are. Once a goal is achieved, things don't stay stable for long. It would be nice, but unfortunately, it doesn't work that way, and I can tell you that at my own expense from direct experience because it has never been so for me.

"You have to advertise!" How many times have you heard that, but what does it mean?

Advertising means reaching the crowd, the audience, and the market through what you do, so you can trigger marketing and sales mechanisms.

What I mean is having a sales message to promote, to get to people, so you can then sell to them.

You have to do it smartly, though. Anyone can create a message, but if it sucks, no one will read it and your money spent on spreading it will be flushed down the toilet. You need to know how to speak to your audience and what they want to hear.

As I mentioned earlier, many aspects need to be taken care of to bring improvement in what you do.

For example, for those who use social media, taking care of photos, videos, and what you write makes all the difference. It's the difference between those who get results and those who don't. Curating doesn't just mean choosing a photo that looks good and matching it with a nice text. Curating means choosing a photo that is attractive to your ideal client accompanied by a text that speaks to him in his language and covers topics that are important to him.

The money you want to make comes from how much care you put into what you do and the value you bring to the market.

I was born on a farm, I'm not saying I'm a farmer because I've never done that job. However, I was born in the country and I know how to grow and harvest.

It's the same principle with business. The money is the fruit to be harvested, and the seeds are our product. If we take care of the soil, the seeds we plant, and the growing process then we will have good fruits to pick up.

It's as simple as that!

Another skill you need to have is the ability to do math.

Advertising, marketing, acquiring customers, and keeping them costs money. You have to be good at figuring out how much money you can really make from selling a product.

To attract new clients, you need large sums of money to create the whole process, and you need to understand whether the proceeds from the sale of the product allow for this expense.

Reaching potential customers is not easy. By now people are bombarded with thousands of information and everyone tells them, "Buy this", "This is the best", "My product is the right one!"...

So, creating an effective message that gets to a fairly large but selected audience of interested people requires a lot of studies, a lot of preparation, and a lot of research. It all adds up to hours and hours paid to experienced people who do just that.

You might say, "Well, I'll study and take care of it!" but it's not that simple. You have to study to be able to properly supervise, but most of the process you'll have to delegate. If you plan on doing everything completely on your own, then good luck!

With all the information you would need to acquire it would take a lot of time, assuming you already understand something about marketing and are not starting from scratch. You'll have to test, try, and make mistakes. This, in addition to time, will waste your money. You could save time and money by simply going to an expert right away and paying him to do the work, that way you start earning money immediately.

What I think the owner of a business or a store should do, is understand how to duplicate sales, and then how to triple them. Knowing marketing for him can be interesting, but he will make more money by delegating this task to people who do it for him.

This means having a successful Business. It means having a system and having people working for you to make the system work so that more money comes into your coffers.

You must have a system that attracts people, converts them into customers, and then leads those customers to buy again and again from you.

The first task is to set up a process that reaches out to potential customers. This process must make you visible so that these prospects learn about your service or product, and the problems you solve. These prospects must perceive what you say and what you do as useful to them, as something that benefits them, helps them, solves a problem for them, gives them solutions, and gives them what they want.

To do all this it is essential to understand what works and what doesn't and to do this it takes tests that require time, a little money, and the appropriate experience to be able to read the results of the tests.

To get your message across effectively, you need to reach potentially interested people, you need to get them to see you, and you need to promote yourself.

Your promotional message must include at least 3 elements:

- Information

- Offer

- Call to action

These three elements must form a process that leads the potential client to understand what you do, to know you, and to know what you do. They need to understand because it is this understanding that will lead them to purchase your products.

Just a little disclaimer on something that often confuses the entrepreneurs I work with. "Offer" doesn't mean a discount. It's what you are offering to your target audience to solve their problems, packed up attractively so that your prospects can't refuse it.

Having a system to acquire customers is much more complex than how some "experts" in the field want to sell it to you. They tell you for personal gain that the system works miracles, but to perform these miracles some aspects need to be taken care of.

First, it is very important to understand the fundamental role of your product or service. Before you do anything and risk throwing money away, you need to understand if what you are selling really serves your target market. Do they really need to solve that problem? Are they willing to pay to solve it?

You need to analyze whether your product or service is presented in the right way, how it is positioned, how your competitors are positioned, and what your product does differently from others. What it actually does demonstrably, not just because you say so. In short, there is a preliminary study to be done that is more important than anything that comes after. The results of the process always depend in a very large part on how well this first phase of analysis is done.

You can be really good at making videos, posts, and ads on social media, but if you don't do a good preliminary study of the product, the market, and the people who make up your potential market, your advertising skills are null and void.

You have to give Prospects (potential customers) reasons to act. You have to show them the advantages and benefits, overcome their objections, answer their questions, and present them with offers tailored to their needs. Without a well-done study before you put the process in motion, you cannot meet the needs of your prospects, and the process will not yield results, proving to be a waste of time, money, and energy.

Unfortunately, if you don't study everything behind being able to do these things, and if you don't do it before you put the process in place, you won't get visible results.

A lot of people get confused by an important factor. They see someone getting a result that they like, and they imitate what that person does because they want the same result, but they find that it doesn't work.

Let me give you an example. I train in martial arts, as I already mentioned. Online there are so many videos that explain how to do certain techniques, how to move, and how to act.

I, who practice regularly, know very well that I need contact with another person to understand, perceive certain reactions from my opponent, and then react accordingly.

There are many factors that I cannot perceive by watching a video. One of these is the muscular perception to be used in a technique because it is something that can only be understood in contact with another person.

I assure you that watching it and then repeating it on your own is absolutely not the same thing as applying it to a person. There is so much information that you can't grasp just by looking at it, but you can only acquire it by direct contact.

The point of my example is that if you copy someone, you can only see the surface work. You can't see the strategic, much bigger, and important one that lies deep inside. So, you can't get the same results unless the person involved explains to you exactly everything that's behind it, all that you can't see by looking at it from the outside.

Now, I'd like to go a little deeper and analyze how you could improve what you do in your business.

The first step is to figure out how to use marketing to bring ideal customers into your business in a predictable way.

You need to structure a system that will go out and get the ideal potential customers for your business. To create the right process to put into practice you need to start from the end i.e. the goal you want to achieve. Most people focus on the starting point of the process. It is thought that this is the starting point for setting up your strategy, but it is not. The starting point is different depending on the goal you want to achieve.

To best create the next stages of the process, it is necessary to carefully study your product and know it very well. You need to know what it does, what solutions it offers, what problems it solves, who it is for, and who it is not for.

Then you have to know your potential client very well. This is important because we cannot promote our product to everyone. Promoting it to everyone would take too many resources in terms of time and money, so it is necessary to focus and target only our ideal customers. This focus will ensure that we maximize our efforts and leave out all those who do not interest us. It is an important skimming exercise to maximize your advertising investment. Efficient marketing is based on the exclusion of those customers we are not interested in. It's a common thought that marketing is based on inclusion but the truth is it's exactly the opposite. You have to choose your customers and exclude all the others from your marketing efforts to maximize your returns on investment.

We need to put our product in front of our ideal customers, those who already have an interest in our product or service. Through the marketing process, you can go and select exactly this type of people.

It is also important that these people want to spend money and we need to prepare them for this with our marketing process. Our product must be attractively presented and must arouse interest in the person so that they want to spend their money on it.

As I just mentioned, you have to choose the people you want to do business with. For example, if I have a product that costs $3,000 and I want to sell it to someone that can hardly afford to spend $1,000, how can I expect to make such kind of sale? If I don't choose my customers I will be disappointed by the lack of sales and results. In this case, the problem with the lack of sales is that I was the one who approached the wrong target audience. I approached a person with a spending capacity incompatible with my product.

It is really possible to implement all the measures I have described so far to bring a big improvement to your business. Start by studying your clientele very well. Who the people are, what habits they have, where they live, what ideas they have about your product, what attitude they have towards the solution you are offering, and much more. Draw up a very precise, complete, and rich in details picture because it will be your most useful tool for making the best decisions in your marketing.

Once you have a detailed analysis of all the elements described so far, you can put together your marketing plan.

Last but not least, once your marketing plan is up and running, you will need to make sure that all aspects of the sales process are well taken care of to achieve significant financial results. The sale is the last step in your marketing process.

You have to take care of the place where you make the sale, whether it is a physical place or an online store. You have to take care of who you sell the product or service to, the image of the person that does the actual sales (he or she represents the image of your business to the customers' eyes), and also the way the sales take place. Again, this applies to both online and offline because in physical businesses you have the salesperson, but you might have a phone salesperson for your e-commerce, a customer service person for your website, or even a website non very intuitive to use. This list could go on and on and may vary slightly based on the type of business, so focus on the sales stages in your business and make sure each is performing at the top of its game.

All of these aspects need to be put into a system designed specifically for a given business, you can't just wake up in the morning and decide what to do.

Businesses and activities that work have a studied and engineered system. A system designed in detail specifically for a given product, for a given audience, and for that specific business or activity.

There is no such thing as a situation that brings results that is out of the blue. Sometimes we are made to believe that it is so, but I can assure you that those who make money have a well-researched system behind them.

Doing marketing is an investment for your business, you should not see it as an expense. Of course, if you do things improvised or blown up, if I do not know what you're doing, or do things just for the sake of doing them, then it all comes down to a simple unnecessary expense rather than an investment.

Step 5: Loyal Recurring Customers

There is a famous book, transcription of a sales talk, called "Acres of Diamonds". It tells the story of a who sells his farm to travel the world in search of diamonds to become rich. He goes in search of wealth without ever finding it and he comes to a tragic end.

The man who bought the farm of the one who left in search of diamonds one day discovers that the property is full of diamonds, they can be easily found everywhere, and the farm is a source of incredible wealth. The previous owner had never seen a diamond so he never recognized the ones laying on the grounds of the farm.

The moral of this story is that we often look left and right for ways to make more money when we have it right under our noses without seeing it or recognizing it.

What do I mean by that? I mean that money is already there and you just need to bend and pick it up. It's in your current customers it's just that you can't see it yet.

You are always only focused on acquiring new customers and those who have already bought fade into the background almost forgotten.

This idea has to be seen from a dedicated perspective, depending on the type of business you have, and how it works.

As I specified earlier, I will not be able to cover all the topics in-depth in this book, but I can give a clear idea of what I mean.

Let us take for example a business that works at its best with repeated purchases in short terms of time from the same customer. Restaurants, hairdressers, beauty salons, and similar businesses, for example. For these types of businesses repeated purchases are key elements. Unfortunately, it is not certain that someone who has purchased once in a certain place, will purchase again in that same place. If I go and get my hair cut at the barber around the corner, I might not go there again when I need a new haircut. I may get a better offer elsewhere or better treatment. I need a good reason to keep going back to the same place.

By this criterion, most business owners focus their marketing on acquiring new customers to keep revenue stable. Of course, we have said in the previous pages how important this is and it is but it is not the only element. Keeping customers is just as important. Every business owner needs to be aware of his own "Acre of Diamonds"

Why don't we find a way to make sure that a customer that has already bought will repeat his purchases? Why don't make sure that he or she buys from us only again and again?

There are two currents of thought regarding the relationship between an existing customer and the business where he has done the purchase. Some owners think that once the business has acquired the customer, he or she will remain attached to the business no matter what, and will continue to buy in the same place again and again.

Other owners think that an acquired customer means nothing special and that you have to keep finding new ones to stay in business.

Who is right? Both! You have to find the right balance between the two tendencies.

In this regard, it is very important to analyze your business and understand what kind of buying process the typical customer of your business does have. You have to understand whether the customers are recurring, whether your product or service is for recurring customers, how recurring these purchases are or can be, and so on.

The key thing is that once you understand this recurring customer buying pattern, you have to use it to better manage them, and keep them coming back.

Let's make an example. You have a business that has customers that return once a month to buy your product. (If you have a business where the customer returns on a broader time basis, years, for example, the argument gets a little more complicated but is still applicable).

You take it for granted that the customer comes back because according to you it has always been that way and, therefore, will always be that way.

You go on with your beautiful business, but one day you notice that sales are down. You tell yourself it is such a period, but it goes on for 3 to 6 months or more. This leads you to cut costs, the few remaining customers notice the situation, they don't accept the trade-off of declining quality, and leave you as well.

Eventually, you are forced to close the business.

One day wandering around your area you notice a new place, the same business as the one you had. It is full of people and you go in for a look and to check it out. The place is nice, but nothing special. The service is good, but nothing special. You buy something to try to understand why it is so busy. At the checkout, they offer you a 20% discount if you leave them your phone number. You accept, take the discount, and leave your number. You start to think that they won't last long with all those discounts.

The next day you get a message thanking you for becoming their customer. The message also says that if you return to the store within 7 days and bring a friend with you they will give you a 50% discount because they want to reward you for becoming their customer. You don't need anything, but the offer is so interesting that you decide to go and take a friend with you. You both end up by something. Here is an extra two purchases that wouldn't have existed without them taking your phone number. By the way, percentages are just for the sake of the example, every promotion or offer needs always been well calculated. You don't need to offer a discount but you surely need to give them something in exchange for their personal information.

How does this buying experience make you feel?

I'll explain what happened if you haven't figured it out yet.

If you don't take care of your customers your competition will do it for you, and take them all away!

It is essential to cultivate good relationships with your customers. You must nurture these relationships and carry them forward over time.

Your customers have already tried your services or products, and obviously, if your product meets expectations, you will have happy and satisfied customers.

Because of these assumptions now those people trust you and your products, they trust your company.

Trust is crucial in customer relationships. If they do not trust you, your product, and your business, they will not buy from you.

The moment they have made their first purchase you will be one step ahead. In fact, you can offer new sales, but you must remember to nurture the relationship with them through calls, texts, emails, and gifts. You can't take the relationship for granted and you can't leave anything to chance, because the moment you do that you risk losing everything the moment someone new comes on the scene.

Once you understand that selling your product repeatedly to people who have already bought it is a gold mine not to be taken for granted, you have to create a marketing process to devote to this category.

The starting point for being able to set this whole process in motion is the creation of a customer list. This starting point is critical if you want to improve your business and your revenue. As soon as a customer buys something from you, he or she must join your list. As we said in Step 4, you acquire a new customer, and the moment they buy you put them on this list, you cannot afford to lose sight of them, and leave them to your competitors.

So, you must have a list of your customers, you must have it written on a computer, and then printed out in physical copy.

This customer list must contain a lot of detailed information about each individual customer. Not just biographical information such as first name, last name, address, email, and phone number, but also more personal information that will allow us to categorize him. For example, what habits he has, what he does he do for a living, and how much he earns. Just gather as much information as you can because it will give you a clearer picture of your customer.

This list of information must be accurate because you need it to understand what kind of person you are dealing with and therefore what action is most effective to take to remind him that he needs to come and buy from you again and again. This fact of reminding him that he must come and buy from you is very important. If you do not take this step you will leave the choice up to the customer as to where and when to buy and definitely that it's not profitable for you.

Your customer, if caught in a moment of weakness, may end up making the wrong choice and going to your competitors, because he may be charmed by fictitious or nonexistent promotions, which, however, appear to him quite good at that time. Unfortunately, once he has made the decision to buy elsewhere, it is not at all easy to get him to come back to you.

That is how your customers start a new relationship with your competitors. It is only because you have somehow neglected them, just as it happens in any other kind of relationship. If you neglect the other party, it goes and seeks attention elsewhere. You have to constantly keep in touch with your customers to continuously improve your relationship.

Let's look at what I think is the minimum information you need to gather to best manage this relationship:

- First name
- Last name
- Phone Number
- Home address

- Email

- Purchase history

- Frequency of purchase

- Purchasing habits

- Date of birth

Once you start to have a large database of data from your already-purchasing customers, you need to start creating systems to keep in touch with them both online and offline. To have a process that produces results and always works, you need to implement those strategies that allow you to stay close to your customer and make them feel part of something, in this case, part of your business. For people in general, a sense of belonging to something is crucial. Take for example sports team fans, for them, the team is so important because they feel part of it, part of something, and you need to be able to replicate that same feeling in your customers to the advantage of your business.

If you don't have a system that allows you to stay in touch with your customers and remind them that they have to come and buy from you, you are bound to be stressed every time you raise the shutter because you don't know if anyone is going to come in today and, therefore, if you are going to make money. You don't know if your customers have decided to abandon you or stay with you.

Let's look at some tips I can give you to succeed in collecting data from your customers.

When a new customer arrives at your business for the first time the person who receives him or her, the Receptionist usually, has to take all possible data on a paper form or on a computer (you will still have to then enter all the data on a computer to sort and organize them). The new customer will also have to sign up for the mailing list in exchange for a freebie or gift. This will make the new customer already feel special and let him know that he is in a special place.

Remember that to use the customer's information for business purposes, you must have a clause for the customer to read, agree to, and sign on the paper sheet. You can also do this directly online, he has to read the clause, accept it through one or more ticks, and add a digital signature.

Once the data is taken, the marketing process can start.

You should keep in touch with your customers at least 10 to 20 times a year. Phone them, send them emails, send thank-you cards for their purchases, paper letters or birthday cards, coupons for them, their spouse, or a friend, and so on. Find ways to always remind them that they are special to you and invite them to come back to your business.

You also need to create a loyalty program to strengthen and increase your relationship with the customer. This is very important because customers who are within a loyalty program spend more money and tell their friends about it. They feel accepted as part of something, they stand up for you if someone speaks ill of you, and they differentiate you from your competitors because they perceive that you are superior to others. To your customer this means everything.

If you propose a purchase to a customer who is in a loyalty program, a customer that often receives communications, freebies, and purchase incentives from you, he will accept almost anything you propose before everybody else does. This allows you to stabilize your cash flow because you have loyal customers who make recurring purchases.

You may be thinking that setting this whole system in motion will take time and money. That's true but you can delegate it and you can automate most of it. Once you do, this will increase your return on the money spent on marketing and you can take care of doing other things, just occasionally overseeing the system.

Basically, you will have to devise a system that, thanks to the data you collect, will keep customers over time and incentivize them to keep buying from you.

At this point, you should have realized that it is critical to keep in touch with your customers because if you don't nurture them, your competition will nurture them for you.

You will have to research what is the best solution for you and apply it. You will have to do some testing and trials, or the person you delegate the process to will have to do it. Test which solution your clients like best, which they respond to most enthusiastically, and which brings you the most profit. I have testimony from my clients that just by sending physical Christmas and birthday cards to their customers, they have achieved so high monetary results that they talk about me and my business to their acquaintances, causing them to become my clients in turn.

All of these tips that I am sharing with you, I have experienced firsthand for myself, and my clients.

I would like to share with you a couple of situations that have happened to me personally that may be useful examples. Several years ago occurred an event in one business I owned and that event made me think.

My granddaughter had just been born, but because of various responsibilities I had, I could not drop everything and go to see her in the hospital. So, I arranged my daily schedule in a way that I leave work at a certain time and go to celebrate. At the last minute, one person asked for my help. Nothing in particular, but it would prevent me from reaching my family. I pointed out that if the need was real I would gladly help him, otherwise, I would go to celebrate.

That person on the spot apologized, but he needed my presence and I stayed.

After a week a nice bottle of wine arrived in my office to thank me, sent by the person I helped that night.

The fact that I did an undue favor made the other person feel indebted to me. Then, of course, he became a loyal customer and stayed for a long time.

On another occasion, I had purchased a car, and when I picked it up, the dealership made me find it under a nice red cloth with a bottle of Champagne inside.

Of course, when I changed cars in subsequent years, I always went to that same car dealer, and, when I had to recommend a dealership, I always mentioned theirs.

If you provide different types of services, people who have already bought from you are more likely to buy other services as well rather than go elsewhere.

The hair salon that offers both cutting and color services comes to mind as an example.

The client who usually cuts her hair at your place may one day be interested in changing color. She will not look around for the best colorist, but she will use the services offered where she usually goes to get her hair cut.

Thus, a client well-taken care of is a client who is more likely to spend money in that same place.

You have to focus on the concept of the economic confidence of customers. They have to keep buying from you, you have to be the first solution that comes to their mind as soon as they think of that product or service. If you don't do it, your competitors will. Remember, it only takes a moment! Your customer sees a new product, the person promoting it is very good, and that customer who was coming to you goes somewhere else, even if the product is poorer, uglier, and less effective.

I see it happen every day, it's less rare than you think. Then I hear from a business owner that things are not going well, that customers have dropped, and various complaints.

I prefer to be always in control of my business, instead of leaving things up to fate, and keeping in touch with current customers is a good way to do that.

At this point, what you need to do is have an organized list of your clients and customers with all the information you need.

The more detailed this list is, the better. Try to get as much information as you can. Think about your customers and write down the main characteristics: what they do for a living, where they live, what habits they have, if they are interested in any particular thing, and if they have any hobbies other than perhaps those inherent to your business, how often they buy, how much they spend, and any useful information you can glean.

You need all this to create appropriate messages to send to your customers to keep in touch.

You need to remember that it is not your customer's job to remember to come to your business, your store, or your site. It is your job to remind him or her to come to you.

There is so much competition that it only takes a little bit for a customer to be captivated by a better message than yours and want to try your competition.

What do I mean by a better message? I can think of a few examples as simple as car commercials. How many times do you see an advertisement that indicates a price that you perceive to be low for a certain car? They show you a picture or a video of a nicely finished car, they show you an incredibly low price, and, by association, you think you can have that car at that price even though the voice or the advertising text never said you could.

Usually, then, there is in small letters an asterisk that says "Price starting from $ ... (that figure)." But few people notice it and many instead run to that dealership to take a look.

It is also critical to stay in touch with your customer to prevent possible teasing.

For example, if you have a dealership and you are on good terms with your customer, when he sees an advertisement that interests him like the one described above, the first thing he does is to call or visit you to ask if you too can offer the same benefits. You will have to warn him about the advertising misunderstanding and make your proposal to him.

Now, let's review in detail the minimum data you must have, in my opinion, to maintain contact:

- First name

- Last name

- Home address

- E-mail address (the main and most commonly used)

- Phone number

And those fundamental to understanding what message to structure:

- Purchase history

- Purchasing habits

- What kind of service do they do when they come to you (if you sell services)

- What products do they buy (if you sell products)

- Date of birth

- What job do they do

- When they take their paycheck (this one may seem trivial to you, but if you send them the right offer on paydays you will see a much higher closing rate. If you check the paydays of most of your customers you will notice that they correspond to your highest collecting days).

If you have all this data you will be able to package an accurate sales message tailored to your type of customer.

I would like to conclude this chapter by further reinforcing the idea that if you want to improve your business and increase your sales you must work on your current customers. This all sounds like a lot of work, and it is, but it must be done.

Remember also that if you want to make more money you have to improve your product and service and you have to make sure you get it in front of the interested people. If you know who your sales message is aimed at you will get more attention and you will be able to sell more to people who listen to you and trust you, your product, and your service.

Out there, entrepreneurs often take too many things for granted. For example, they take it for granted that a person has to buy from them, but I hope I have made you realize that this is very far from reality in today's market. There is so much choice out there that people buy wherever they like, so the entrepreneur's certainty that they should buy from him is based on nothing.

These owners who take everything for granted are the same ones who complain that they have no more customers and then close their business.

Take my advice and do what others are not doing, you will be surprised.

Chapter 9

How to Improve the Process

Now, I want to share with you a couple of tips for improving the whole marketing process to acquire and retain customers.

The first tip I want to share with you is to **_be visible_** as much as possible.

If you want people to buy from you, you have to make yourself visible, and you have to reach the people you are interested in reaching. As you should have understood by now, I advocate the fact that you have to study and act. If you don't study, if you don't know your product, your market, and the people you want to reach you will never understand how to interest them. To reach them you have to know them, know what they want, how they talk, what they fear, what problems they have, and what they want. The more you know about them, the easier it will be for you to attract their attention, talk to them, and give them what they want. If you have yet to create your product or service, even better. If you know your audience really well, you can create the perfect product for them, and then you will make really stellar sales.

To sell, though, they have to know you, they have to know you exist, and they have to know your product or service and your company.

You have to take your message to them and you have to make sure that the message gets to them, and they hear it. You have to win their attention despite all the noise in the market today.

Don't be like those who wait at the door for the customer to come in because that doesn't work anymore. You have to be the one to go get the customer, we are in an era in which we are just a "Click" away from everything, you can have anything with one click, and now everyone comes to your house with any service with just one click.

If you don't allow people who are looking for your product to find you, you will be cut off. There are no more excuses, those who are not active in the process of going to customers, within a short time are destined to close.

It's not just me saying this for the sake of saying it or to scare people off, just look around you. Businesses are closing at an impressive rate, and the reason, as obvious as it may be, is always the same, they don't have enough customers. Business owners that end unclosing down complain that there are no more customers around.

On the other hand, when you talk to someone who has a business that works well, who has a customer acquisition system in place, and a system to retain customers, well, they tell you a different story. They will tell you that there is plenty of customers, you just have to go look for them and be very good at keeping them once found.

If you want to look the other way and close your eyes, that's fine. That's your choice but I don't agree with this way of dealing with things, and I don't respect it.

Just look around you, many businesses are increasing their revenue every year in exactly the same industry as the one you are in.

With that being said, you should understand that if someone has succeeded it means you can succeed too. The problem is probably that you still have not figured out what is not working in your business. Always remember that the solution to a problem already exists, you just don't see it yet. If you still don't see it after all you've read so far, go back and read Step 1: **"Mindset"** over and over again. You need to change the way you look at things to see the same things differently. This is how you can see what has not been working for you so far.

In conclusion, my first suggestion is to give yourself a chance by reaching out to those prospects who might want to buy your product, service, or solution.

My second suggestion is to **_learn how to sell_**!

What does learning to sell mean to me? It means knowing who my customers are, knowing how to communicate with them, knowing what problems they have, and studying solutions to help them.

Study, apply, study, apply, and then study and apply. You never stop learning! If you don't have time yourself to learn how to sell hire someone to do it for you, look for those who can help you sell more and better.

Waiting for the customer to decide whether or not to buy is not an effective strategy. I'm not saying to be nagging with customers, that's not selling, that's nagging.

What I mean is selling without seeing. You have to know your potential customers so well that you can help them get from point A to B, that is, get them from where they are to where they want to go, through your product or service. To do that you have to know everything about them. You need to their weaknesses, their strengths, what they want, how they want it, what keeps them up at night, and so on. The salesperson's job is to create a system around these customers that helps them to choose so that with your product they can get what they want. To use the words we used before, with your product or service they have to go from A, where they are, to B where they want to go. A good salesman can do this with no problem and you need good salesmen to take good care of your customers.

Chapter 10

What to Do Now?

Now it's time for action! I want you to take a pen and a piece of paper and start writing down your system. Your description should include the strategies you use both to acquire new customers and retain current ones.

Take an hour or two of your time and start writing down the whole process your customers go through. Start with how they get to know you and go all the way to how you make them come back to buy more.

Write down how you reach your prospects, how you communicate with them, and what you communicate. Proceed to list all the steps until you get to the sale, which is when they give you money, and you say goodbye to them. Be clear, precise, and detailed.

Analyze the list in light of what you have learned in this book and make some adjustments to test where needed. Don't you have a way to reach your prospects? Build one! Don't you know the best way to communicate with them? Learn how!

Now, you have all the tools you need to work on your system and fix what isn't working. If you are thinking that you don't have a process at all, I disagree with you. You most definitely do have a system. Probably you didn't build it and it built itself on causality, that's why you don't know about it. Try to look at your business to trace it back. If you can't see it at all, build one from scratch and start implementing it right away, using the knowledge acquired so far.

This is the point where you will understand if you have wasted your money and time by buying this book.

If you are reading these lines and you are thinking, "Yes, I'll do it later, I don't feel like it now!" or "I have something else to do now. I don't have time for this", you know very well deep inside you that these are just excuses to procrastinate. You need to re-read very well Step 3: "**Act**".

If, on the other hand, you are already in action and you are writing your list, I congratulate you. You are one of the few people who have figured out how it works, one of the top 10% of people who acts on the new information acquired.

Writing down the whole process, even if you don't have one and are just making it up from scratch, is very important. It makes you understand the fundamental role of each one of the various steps behind a successful business process.

This is a very important exercise because it allows you to analyze every step in the process of your business, that process that leads people to spend their money on your business.

Let me underline once more that if you think you don't have a process right now, you are wrong. The process is necessarily there, just you are not in control of it.

You have to be in control of the process of customer acquisition and management because that allows you to make revenue forecasts. Revenue forecasting allows you to design the new things you can do with the money coming in. If you are in control of the process you can also eliminate any eventual wrong phase. For example, if after analyzing very well, you find that one phase of the process makes you spend more money than the one it brings in, you can cut that phase without looking back.

After you finish the first list I suggested, you need to do the same with your existing customers. Analyze the process you use to tell them they have to come back and buy from you again and possibly more. Again write down a very clear and detailed list.

Describe how you invite them to come back for more, what you do to sell more products (upsell and cross-sell options), how you spoil them to show how important they are to you, and so on. It might be you do not have a process that sells more products or more expensive products to your existing customers, that's what is usually called upsell or cross-sell system depending on the case. I strongly recommend that you get it in place as quickly as possible because it brings amazing benefits to the income of any business.

After reading this book I hope you have understood what a great resource current customers are. Treat them well and maintain good and healthy relationships with them. By doing so, you will have great value in return, technically called the "Lifetime Value" of a customer.

Conclusion

We have come to the time for goodbyes.

I would like to thank you for reading my book and getting to the end.

I am sure that you and I will meet again, maybe in another book, maybe we will do business together because your business needs professional help, or maybe in some other circumstance. If you want to keep in touch just visit my website:

www.azionebusiness.com

The website is in Italian which is my main market. Even though, I have many English-speaking customers, so you can contact me in English. Just click on the icons on the site of Messenger or Whatsapp, whichever you prefer, leave me your message, and I will be more than happy to help you with my answer.

Good luck and have a great life,

Alessio

www.ingramcontent.com/pod-product-compliance
Lightning Source LLC
Chambersburg PA
CBHW050258120526
44590CB00016B/2403